Polar Animals

and Other Cold-Climate Creatures

By
Pascale Hédelin

Illustrated by
Didier Balicevic
Maëlle Cheval
Yating Hung
Yi-Hsuan Wu

Twirl

Contents

The Mountains in the Winter 70

Index 92

On the Ice and in the Water 48

? The "Let's Review!" pages at the end of each section help reinforce learning.

Index Quickly find the word you're looking for with the index at the end of the book.

Look for the colored boxes in the bottom right-hand corners. You will find references to related subjects in other parts of the book.

Frozen Lands of North America

Cold-Climate Regions

The North and South Poles have freezing temperatures all year long. Other parts of the world might be cold only in the winter.

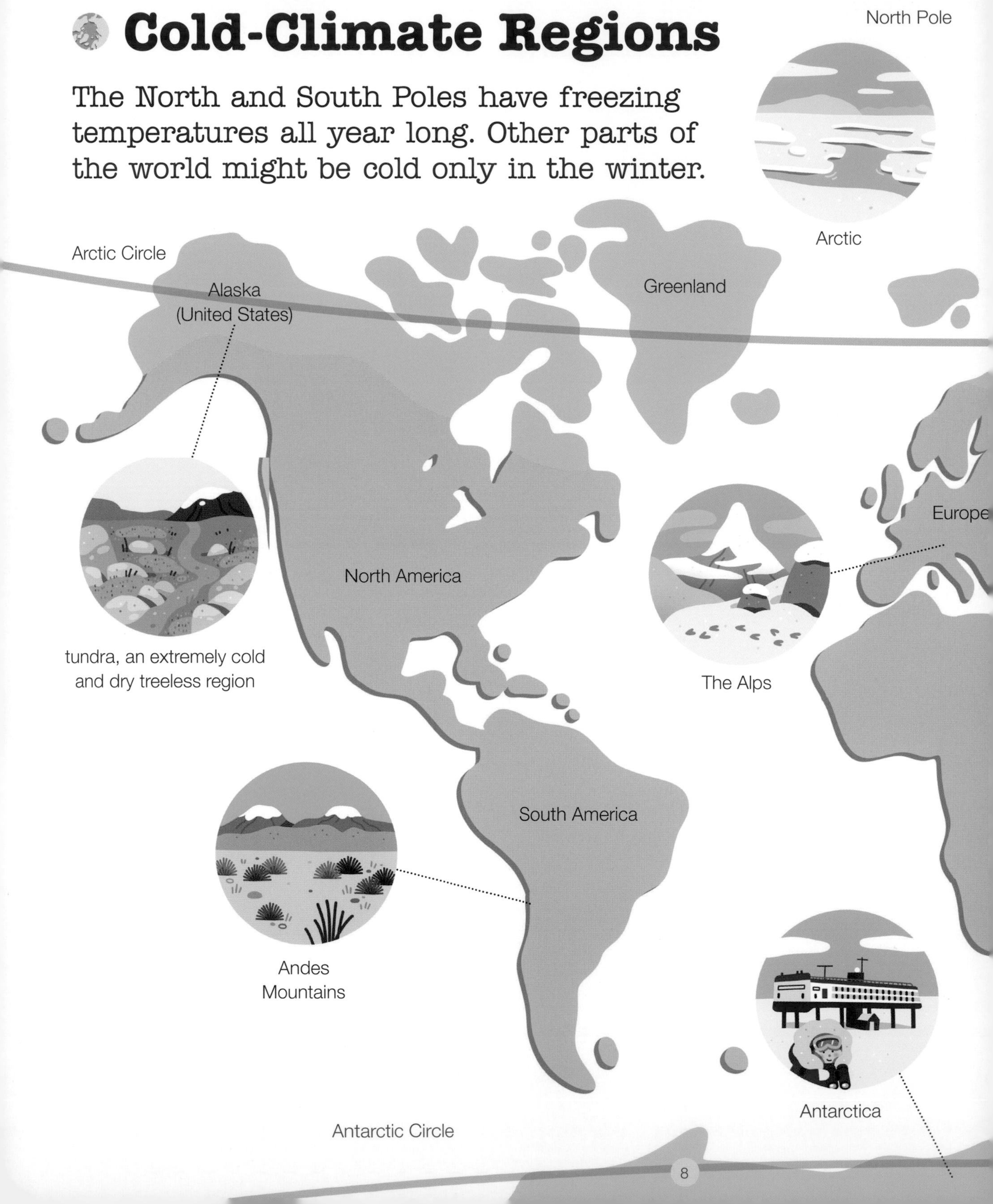

North Pole

Arctic

Arctic Circle

Alaska
(United States)

Greenland

North America

Europe

tundra, an extremely cold
and dry treeless region

The Alps

South America

Andes
Mountains

Antarctica

Antarctic Circle

boreal (meaning northern) forests, or taigas

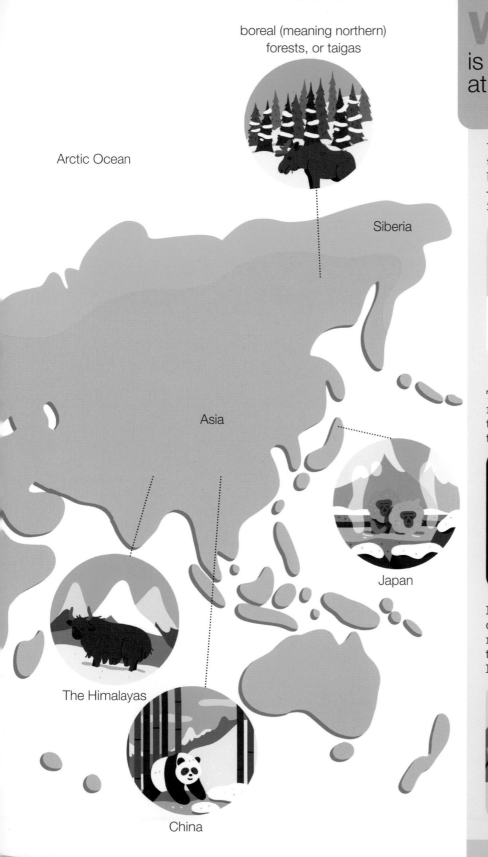

Arctic Ocean

Siberia

Asia

Japan

The Himalayas

China

You would definitely shiver in the Arctic in the winter. It's between −4 and −40°F (−20 and −40°C) there! And in the summer, it doesn't get above 50°F (10°C).

The poles are colder than other regions in the world because they receive less sunlight over the course of the year.

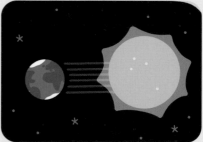

Hot-climate regions, on the other hand, get sunlight all year round. In Cameroon, Africa, the average temperature in February is around 86°F (36°C).

🏠 Cold Regions in North America

Winters are long and harsh in Alaska and northern Canada. Much of the ground is frozen, and people and animals have adapted to living in this climate.

sled dogs

arctic wolf

musk ox

arctic fox

snowpack

silver birch

lichen

caribou

arctic hare

snowy owl

Arctic tundra

grizzly bear

frozen ground

Inuit people

snowmobile

houses on stilts

drying fish on racks

lemming

Why
do Inuit people build igloos

?

The Inuit people used to move around on dogsleds to look for food. They hunted for seals or fished for salmon.

During their journeys, they would stop to build igloos with blocks of snow. These provided shelter for a few days.

Today, snowmobiles often replace dogsleds, and the Inuit people live in permanent wooden homes.

In a Blizzard **18**
An Arctic Night **24**

🦌 Caribou

A member of the deer family, caribou are well adapted to the cold. They are always on the move, in search of food.

large antlers

thick winter coat

furry tail

long legs

broad, furry hooves that walk easily on ice and snow

Calves are born in the spring.

Males lose their antlers in the fall. Females shed theirs in spring.

New antlers appear on males in late winter; in late spring for females.

living in a herd

eating lichen

swimming in cold waters

using antlers to defend against a wolf

These two animals look a lot alike because they're the same animal!

In North America, the animal is called a caribou if it's wild, and a reindeer if it's domesticated. In Europe and Asia, they are known as reindeer.

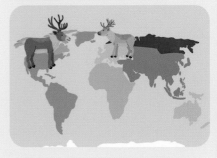

Reindeer herding is a tradition of the Sámi people in northern Europe. They move with the reindeer as the animals search for shelter and fresh food.

Arctic Wolf **14**
Migrations **26**

Arctic Wolf

Awoooo! Also known as the polar wolf or white wolf, the arctic wolf lives and hunts in packs.

two layers of fur

white coat

sharp teeth

eating snow for water

wolf pups waiting for food

den

14

hunting a
caribou

stalking a hare

Why
do we call it the big bad wolf ?

With their big teeth, wolves may look a little scary. And the sound of their howls, which they use to communicate, can also be alarming.

In fairy tales, the wolf is often described as a fierce and dangerous character who causes harm to people.

Wolves are apex predators, and they hunt for their food, but in reality, the risk of wolves attacking humans is low. They usually avoid people.

In a Blizzard **18** ❄
Migrations **26** ♫

Birds of the Tundra

Few birds spend the winter here. But some are able to survive the cold because they have two layers of feathers, along with larger bodies and shorter legs.

thick white feathers

male

feathers on legs

talons

female

sharp eyes

snowy owls

eating buds

walking on soft snow

ruffed grouse

feeding on a carcass left
by an arctic wolf

ravens

able to fly, swim,
and walk

searching
for food

snow geese

You may have seen birds building nests in trees. That's where they lay their eggs and raise their young.

Snowy owls don't make nests in trees. In the spring, a female snowy owl will dig a hole on a hill where all the snow has melted, then make a nest in the ground.

Even though temperatures may be very cold, the snowy owl is able to keep her chicks warm by staying close to them.

In a Blizzard **18**
Birds of the Boreal Forest **40**

✳ In a Blizzard

During strong snowstorms called blizzards, the icy wind blows very hard. Animals have different ways of protecting themselves.

icy wind

very thick hair and large amounts of fat

musk oxen: huddling against the wind

ruffed grouse: burrowing under snow

arctic hare: hiding behind a wall of snow

arctic wolves: sleeping close
together to keep warm

snowy owl:
taking shelter
behind a rock

arctic fox:
digging a tunnel

How

does a musk ox protect itself **?**

If you go outside on a cold winter day wearing only a T-shirt and shorts, you will very likely start to shiver! You aren't protected against the cold.

A musk ox is well-protected against the cold because it has two coats: an outer layer of long, shaggy hair, and an inner layer of shorter hairs called qiviut.

When predators approach, musk oxen protect the herd by placing their young in the middle. The adults stand with their horns facing out.

Arctic Fox

This small fox has adapted well to the extreme temperatures of the Arctic region.

small ears

long, bushy tail

burrow

short, pointed muzzle

thick white winter coat

camouflaged in snow

fur turning brown in spring

wrapping its body with its fluffy tail

finding a lemming by using smell and sound

pouncing

fox kits

marking their territory

How
does the size of an arctic fox help it survive ?

You may have seen pictures of a red fox, or even one in real life. The arctic fox is related to the red fox, but it's smaller, about the size of a large pet cat.

Like many cold-climate animals, the arctic fox has short legs, a short muzzle, and small ears. These characteristics help them lose less body heat.

The fennec fox lives in the hot desert, and it needs to release heat from its body to keep cool. Notice how big its ears are!

In a Blizzard **18** ✳
Fur and Feathers **78** 🪶

🦔 Small Creatures

Some little animals are active all winter. Others hibernate, or sleep through the season, in their burrows. There are others that overwinter: They rest but stay active.

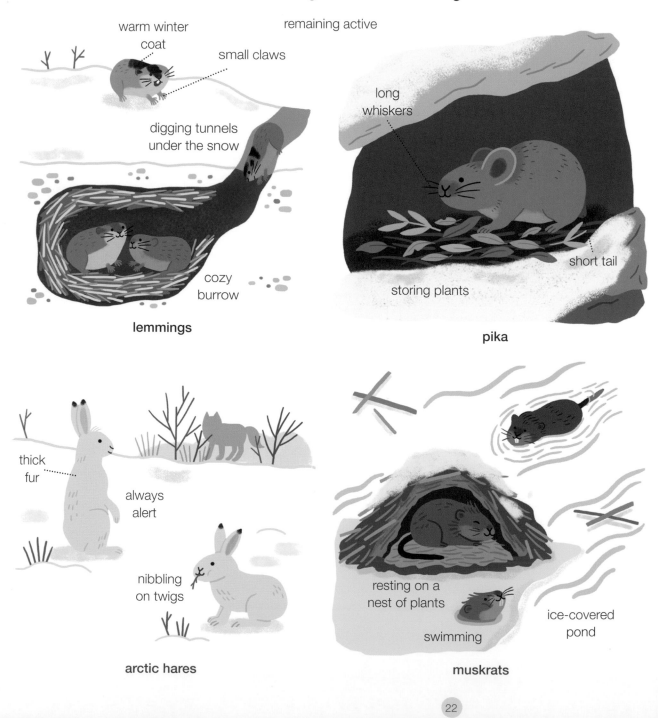

warm winter coat

remaining active

small claws

digging tunnels under the snow

long whiskers

cozy burrow

short tail

storing plants

lemmings

pika

thick fur

always alert

nibbling on twigs

resting on a nest of plants

swimming

ice-covered pond

arctic hares

muskrats

hibernating

burrow

sleeping in
a group

arctic ground squirrels

mostly sleeping, but
waking up once in
a while to eat

burrow

living in
a colony

chipmunks

What
do lemmings
do underground
?

When snow falls, it forms
a layer on the ground that
protects everything that lives
underneath from the bitter cold.
It's like a blanket!

Lemmings spend the winter
sheltering in underground
tunnels with designated spaces
for sleeping and nesting, as well
as toilets.

Their underground burrows keep
these small creatures safe, not
only from the extreme weather,
but also from predators.

Migrations **26**
Hibernating and Overwintering **86**

🔦 An Arctic Night

It's daytime, but it's dark out! During the winter in the Arctic and sub-Arctic regions, it can be dark for six months.

hunters: examining tracks

moose: using its keen sense of smell and hearing

arctic fox: catching prey

caribou: looking under snow for plants

northern lights,
or aurora borealis

sightseers

snowy owl: listening
for its prey

arctic wolf: seeing
well in the dark

arctic hare:
sniffing for
plants to eat

musk ox: digging with
hooved feet to find plants

What
are auroras

?

Sometimes, colorful waves of lights fill the night sky in the regions near the poles. These polar lights are called auroras.

Auroras form when particles from the Sun are pushed by Earth's magnetic field toward the poles. As they hit the gases above Earth, the gases glow.

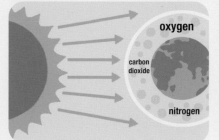

oxygen

carbon
dioxide

nitrogen

You may have noticed another colorful phenomenon that sometimes appears in the sky after it rains. Have you ever seen a rainbow?

Migrations

Animals travel long distances to look for warmer weather or food and water, and to reproduce.

snowy owl: flying south to warmer weather

right whale: migrating to reproduce

lemmings: swimming to look for food

arctic wolves: pursuing caribou

Canada geese: flying south in a V shape

They can fly 620 miles (1,000 kilometers) a day.

caribou: moving toward a boreal forest

traveling in a large group

Arctic foxes are always wandering to find food.

What
animal has the longest migration **?**

Arctic terns are seabirds that are related to gulls. In the summer, they live in the Arctic region, near the North Pole.

In the winter, they fly all the way to Antarctica, completing the longest migration of any animal on this planet!

In each bird's lifetime, the distance it travels from north to south and back again equals two round trips between Earth and the Moon!

Caribou **12**
Small Creatures **22**

Do you know the names of these animals?
How are they protected against the cold?

Can you help the lemming find its way to the right burrow?
Who lives in the other burrows?

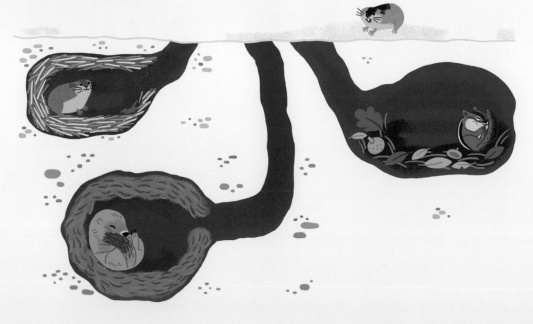

Animals have many ways of protecting themselves during a snowstorm.
What are these animals doing to protect themselves? Look at their techniques
for escaping the icy wind. How might other animals protect themselves?

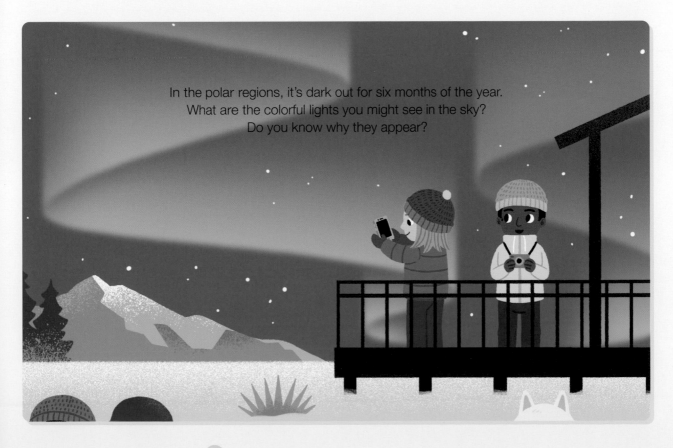

In the polar regions, it's dark out for six months of the year.
What are the colorful lights you might see in the sky?
Do you know why they appear?

Winter
in the Boreal Forest

🌲 The Siberian Forest

In a boreal forest, or taiga, temperatures can fall to −58°F (−50°C). One of the biggest boreal forests in the world is in Siberia, in northern Russia.

fir

Siberian lynx

Amur tiger

long canine teeth

Siberian musk deer

lichen

pine

wooden house

Yakut people

raising **reindeer** and **horses**

frozen road

using a snowmobile to transport hay

wolverine

trapper's cabin

tamarack

brown bear

sable

trapper

river

silver birch

beaver building a dam

cut branches

beaver's lodge

moose

woodcutter cutting down trees

How
do trees survive the cold

Trees in the boreal forest are mostly conifers: pines, spruces, tamaracks, and firs. They are well-adapted to the cold.

Their cone shapes allow snow to slide off, and their needlelike leaves have a wax coating that keeps moisture in and protects against the harsh winds.

The dark green color of the leaves also helps them absorb more sunlight. They freeze less easily than broad-leaved trees, such as oaks and maples.

Brown Bear **36**
Moose **38**

 Wolverine

The wolverine is the largest member of the weasel family. Its scientific name is *Gulo gulo*, which means "the glutton." And it is well-named: It eats everything, even prey much bigger than it is!

powerful jaws

claws

catching its prey

climbing easily

finding shelter in a tree stump

🦦 Other Weasels

sable

soft, shiny coat

digging up food stored for the winter

short tail

broad, furry feet

Siberian weasel

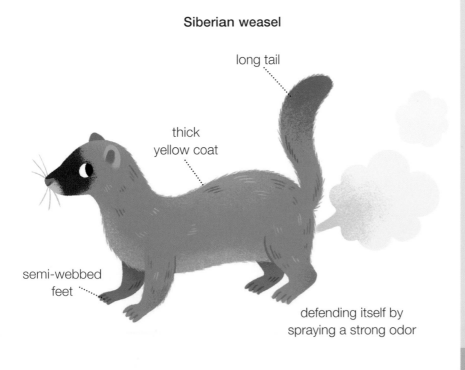

long tail

thick yellow coat

semi-webbed feet

defending itself by spraying a strong odor

What are mink farms ?

The furs of animals such as the mink are sold to make luxury clothing. These creatures were hunted for centuries, almost to the point of extinction.

They were then raised on farms. In countries where mink farms are still legal, mink are kept in extremely poor conditions.

Many countries have since banned these farms, and animal rights organizations worldwide are calling for an end to fur farming.

🐻 Brown Bear

Brown bears spend most of their time by themselves. They explore the boreal forest in search of food, sleep for much of the winter, and take care of their young.

thick fur

large, thin body

broad feet with claws

male

female

in summer

looking for berries

catching salmon

meeting other bears

in winter

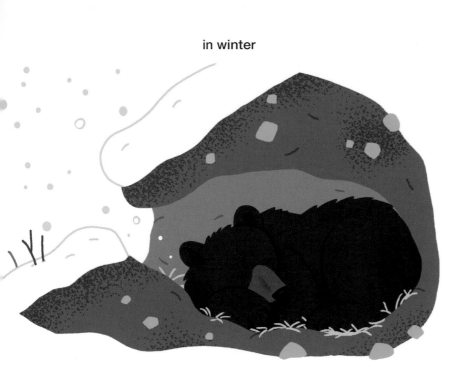

overwintering: mostly sleeping, but waking up every now and then

den

cubs

giving birth to young

What
do brown bears eat
?

You're an omnivore: You eat a little bit of everything. So are brown bears! But they prefer to eat plants.

Their main diet is fruits, seeds, and mushrooms. However, they also feed on ants, fish, deer, and small mammals.

Like tigers, brown bears are apex predators, with no natural predators. A battle between these two animals would be fierce.

Polar Bear **52**
Hibernating and Overwintering **86**

Moose

Moose are the largest members of the deer family. These plant-eating animals can weigh more than 1,000 pounds (450 kilograms)!

huge, flat antlers

dewlap, or bell

male

large feet with hooves

grazing in the water

swimming

Why
do some moose have huge antlers

?

Each male moose grows a new set of antlers every year. These antlers, or paddles, of a full-grown moose can measure about 6 feet (2 meters) across!

Moose use their antlers to defend themselves against predators, as well as other male moose during mating season.

In the winter, the antlers fall off so the moose can conserve energy, and a new set will grow in the spring.

small eyes

eating bark and leaves

sensitive upper lip that can grasp food

calf

taking care of her young

female

Birds of the Boreal Forest

Many types of birds migrate from cold to warm climates before winter arrives. The ones that remain in cold regions look for food and shelter among the trees.

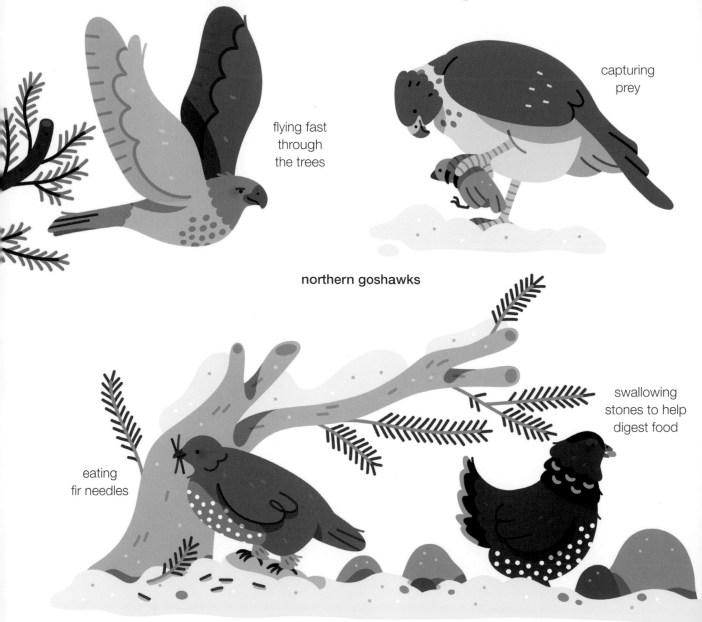

capturing prey

flying fast through the trees

northern goshawks

swallowing stones to help digest food

eating fir needles

toes firmly gripping the snow

Siberian grouse

living in the trees

red crossbills

looking for
seeds

active for three
hours a day

Siberian jays

migrating south

Siberian nuthatch

taiga flycatcher

Birds have all kinds of beaks: small, pointed, rounded . . . These shapes allow each type of bird to grasp their food.

The tips of the crossbill's beak do not meet, but cross at the ends. It can easily open cones of pines, firs, and other evergreen trees to pluck out the seeds.

The crossbill also uses its beak to help it climb. This bird can hang upside down to eat!

Birds of the Tundra **16**
Seabirds **55**

 Amur Tiger

This powerful creature is well protected from the cold by its thick coat, layer of fat, and extra fur around its neck and paws.

lighter coloring in winter

stripes

thick fur

powerful legs

long claws

waiting for prey

muscular body

wild boar

pouncing on its prey

42

Why
are Amur tigers endangered ?

sharpening its
claws by scratching
a tree trunk

cubs

peeing to mark its territory

Amur tigers are the world's biggest cats. An adult male can weigh up to 675 pounds (306 kilograms).

They are endangered because much of their natural habitat has been reduced and they have been illegally hunted for their fur and body parts.

Amur tigers are now a protected species. Nature reserves have even been created to restore their population.

🦉 A Night in the Forest

At night, while some animals are sleeping, others are up and about, in search of food.

red crossbill: sleeps in the tree

wolverine: active day and night, rarely taking shelter

beaver: gnawing on wood

Amur tiger: hunts mostly at night

reindeer

great gray owl: hunting at night

Siberian musk deer: feeding on lichen and leaves

moose: sleeping in the bushes

Siberian lynx

How

is global warming a threat to animals ?

Many human activities, including manufacturing, transportation, and intensive agriculture and livestock farming, have contributed to Earth's warming climate.

If the temperatures in the boreal forest rise to extreme levels, the trees will suffer from disease and many fires will occur.

The destruction of their forest habitat will result in fewer places for animals to find shelter or food. They will try to look for these in areas where people live.

Wolverine **34**

Animals in Danger **88**

The Yakut people live in the boreal forest in Siberia. Can you describe what they are doing in this scene?

Look at this moose: what a giant! Can you name the body parts indicated by the dotted lines? What is a baby moose called? What do moose eat?

The wolverine and the Siberian weasel are members of the weasel family.
What interesting characteristics do each of them have?

The Amur tiger is a large and powerful creature.
How does it protect itself from the cold?

When daylight fades in the boreal forest, some animals go to sleep while others become active.

What do *you* do at night?

On the Ice
and in the Water

The Arctic

This northernmost region, at the North Pole, includes a partially frozen ocean surrounded by land. Many animals live here, on the ice and in the water.

iceberg

melting ice shelf

Steller sea lions

polar bear

auks

narwhal

arctic cod

bowhead whale

ivory gulls

arctic terns

oil rig

icebreaker
ship

belugas

Inuit hunters

kayak

walruses

oil slick

What
is pack ice

?

The surface of a frozen lake is a thick, very hard layer of ice. It keeps the water below at a warmer temperature so marine and plant life don't freeze.

Pack ice is a layer of frozen seawater that is not attached to land. It is 3 to 6.5 feet (1 to 2 meters) thick and floats on the water. You can walk on it!

Arctic animals depend on this sea ice to survive. Walruses raise their young on the ice and rest there in between dives into the water for food.

Polar Bear

Polar bears are the largest bears in the world. They are the only bear species to be considered marine mammals because they spend most of their life on the sea ice of the Arctic region.

two layers of fur to protect from extreme cold

traveling long distances

claws to firmly grip the ice

thick pads on soles of feet to prevent slipping

catching a seal through a hole in the ice

diving into the water
to catch fish

broad, slightly
webbed feet

cubs
playfighting

mother getting
food for her
young

Why
are polar bears "threatened"

?

Polar bears are the top predator in the Arctic region. These powerful creatures need a large territory of pack ice to roam around and hunt in.

Because of global warming, the Arctic sea ice is melting, reducing the polar bears' habitat and food sources, including seals, their main prey.

Polar bears are protected by laws, and certain areas in North America have been designated for them to safely feed, shelter, and grow their population.

The Arctic **50**
Growing Up in the Cold **66**

 Walrus

This very social marine mammal has a thick layer of fat to keep itself warm. It may move awkwardly on land, but it is graceful in the water.

thick skin

sensitive whiskers, or vibrissae, that help locate shellfish

long tusks

flipper

eating shellfish

using its tusks to climb out of the water

walrus herd: packed together on shrinking sea ice

🐧 Seabirds

The water-repellent feathers and thick down of seabirds protect them as they fly and swim to catch their prey.

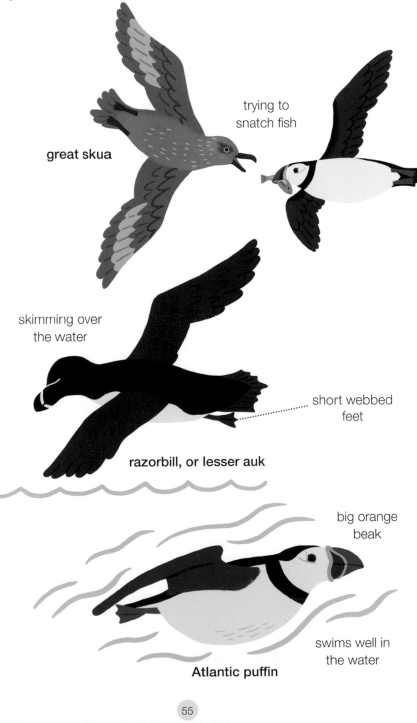

trying to snatch fish

great skua

skimming over the water

short webbed feet

razorbill, or lesser auk

big orange beak

swims well in the water

Atlantic puffin

These two seabirds are often mistaken for each other: they're both black and white, and they live in cold climates.

However, they are two different bird species. Auks can fly, but penguins can't: Their wings are too short and flat.

Auks live between the North Pole and the Mediterranean Sea. Penguins live at the South Pole.

Emperor Penguin **60** 🐧
Growing Up in the Cold **66**

🐋 Cetaceans

These marine animals—which include whales, dolphins, and narwhals—are not fish, but mammals: They breathe in air at the surface and nurse their young.

two blowholes

large head

breaking through
the ice for air

bowhead whale

fluke

krill

white skin
camouflaging
against sea ice

chasing
prey

belugas

octopus

leaping out of the
water to catch prey

blowhole

dorsal
fin

smooth
skin

seal

Orcas live in large
groups, or pods.

spiral tusk

male

narwhals

female

small flippers

Krill is the primary food of
many marine animals, from
large whales to small seabirds.

They are tiny shrimplike
creatures that live in large
groups called swarms. They
eat microscopic algae called
phytoplankton.

Krill are an essential part of the
food web in the ocean. Without
them, the marine ecosystem
would be greatly affected, and
many species would not survive.

Migrations **26**
The Arctic **50**

🏭 Antarctica

This southernmost continent is the coldest place on Earth. There are few animals on the land, but many species live in the water.

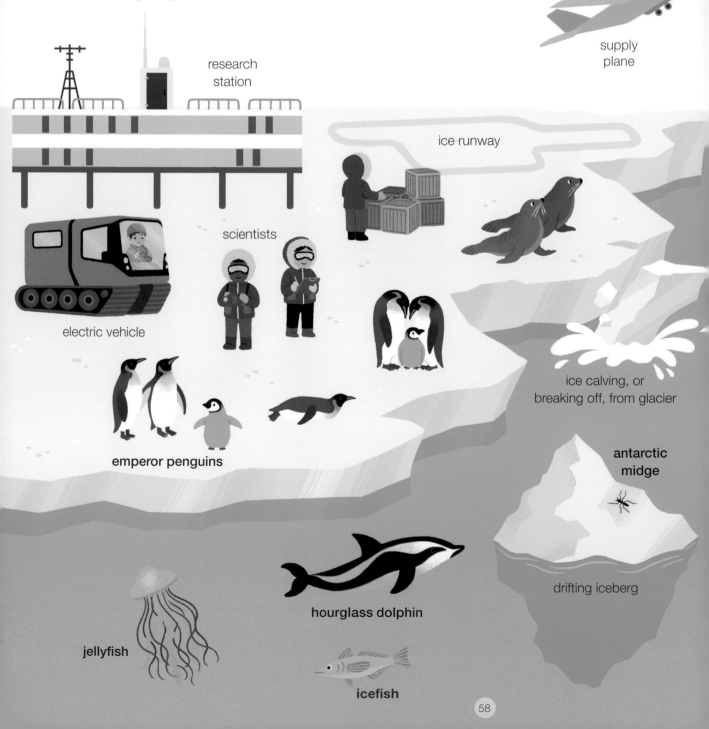

supply plane

research station

ice runway

scientists

electric vehicle

ice calving, or breaking off, from glacier

antarctic midge

emperor penguins

drifting iceberg

hourglass dolphin

jellyfish

icefish

antarctic tern

skua

sightseers

ferry

pack ice

elephant seals

Weddell seal

squid

leopard seal

floating chemicals

The **orca** lives in Antarctica and the Arctic.

While there are no permanent residents here, there are 70 research stations that are staffed by scientists who come from all over the world.

For a few months or a year, the scientists observe the animals, the water, the rocks, and even the air. They dig deep into the ice to analyze air bubbles.

The data collected informs researchers about the climates that Earth has experienced and helps them predict future climate changes.

Emperor Penguin **60**
Weddell Seal **62**

Emperor Penguin

Emperor penguins live only on the Antarctic continent. They gather in colonies, which can have as many as 5,000 penguins!

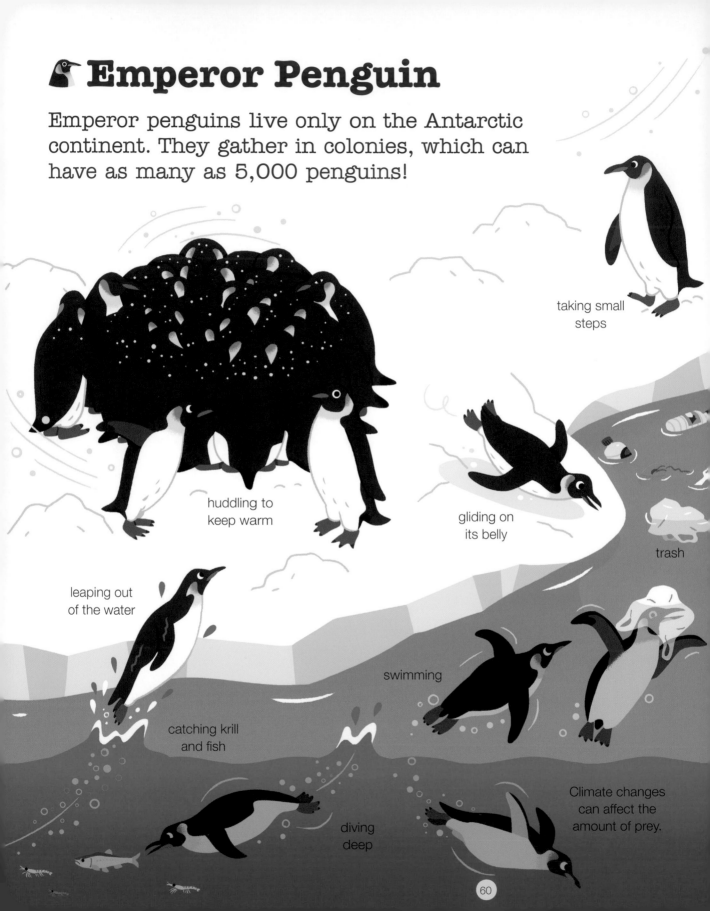

taking small steps

huddling to keep warm

gliding on its belly

trash

leaping out of the water

swimming

catching krill and fish

diving deep

Climate changes can affect the amount of prey.

standing upright

long beak

smooth feathers

rocket-shaped body

small, stiff, flat wing

webbed feet that have feathers and a layer of fat

claws

What

other penguins live in Antarctica

Eight species of penguins live in and around Antarctica. The emperor penguin is the biggest, standing about 45 inches (115 centimeters) tall.

Chinstrap penguins look like they're wearing helmet straps. Magellanic penguins hunt for food in groups, diving deep to catch fish and shrimp.

Rockhopper penguins are easy to recognize by their yellow crests—and by the way they hop from rock to rock!

Seabirds 55
Cetaceans 56

 Weddell Seal

Weddell seals are found mostly in the waters around Antarctica. These mammals have a bulky body and small head. Their diet includes fish, octopus, squid, and shrimp.

sensitive whiskers, or vibrissae

hind flippers

powerful flippers

short, thick fur

diving deep

catching fish

swimming under the ice

making loud noises to warn predators

fleeing from a leopard seal

How
do Weddell seals breathe while in the water ?

Weddell seals swim very well, and can spin around and swim backward. They can also hold their breath and stay underwater for over an hour.

Under the sea ice, the seals can detect where there are natural cracks, but sometimes they have to create breathing holes by using their teeth to break ice.

When they're tired, the seals take a nap. They can sleep upright in the water, with just their heads poking out, or lie on their backs on the ice.

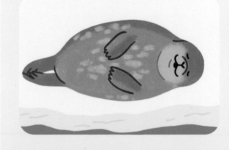

Survival in Extreme Cold **64**
Growing Up in the Cold **66**

Survival in Extreme Cold

The bodies of animals living in Antarctica are equipped to handle the extreme cold temperatures.

thick layer of fat

orca

double layer of fur
and a layer of fat

seal

four layers of
waterproof
feathers

layer of fat
under skin

standing upright
to touch the cold
ground less

emperor penguin

swimming
under the ice

icefish

Butterflies are not able to fly in
extremely cold environments.
They would also be unable to
find flowering plants to gather
nectar from.

However, the antarctic midge
is very resilient. Its larva
spends about nine months of
its two-year life cycle frozen
underground.

The midge is smaller than a pea,
but it is the continent's largest
land animal! When it finally
becomes an adult, it lives for
just ten days.

Growing Up in the Cold

When the animals are born, it takes a while to grow thick fur and develop enough fat to keep safe. They receive warmth and nourishment from their parents until they're ready to go out on their own.

in the Arctic

safe in a den
under the snow

keeping cubs
warm

polar bear and cubs

digging in the
mud for food

staying close to
her young

drinking mother's
nutrient-rich milk

whale and calf

walrus and calf

in the Antarctic

male keeping
the egg warm

female hunting
for fish

egg

emperor penguins

thick gray
feathers

huddling to
keep warm

emperor penguin chicks

waiting for its
mother

light-colored
fur

Weddell seal pup

How
does a
baby seal
handle the cold
?

When it is born, a baby seal is suddenly exposed to the wind and cold of its environment. It doesn't yet have a thick layer of fat like the grown-ups to insulate it.

However, the seal quickly develops the fat layer as it begins to drink its mother's milk. But when rain falls, the seal gets soaked!

To warm up, the baby seal shivers to activate its muscles and create warmth in its body. You do the same thing when you're cold!

Let's Review!

Do you know the names of these two birds?
How are they alike? How are they different?

Pair each adult animal with its young. What are the names of these creatures?

Can you identify the tusks, vibrissae, and flippers of this walrus? Does it move easier on land or in the water?

Which of these creatures are the predators, and which are the prey? Do you remember who eats whom?

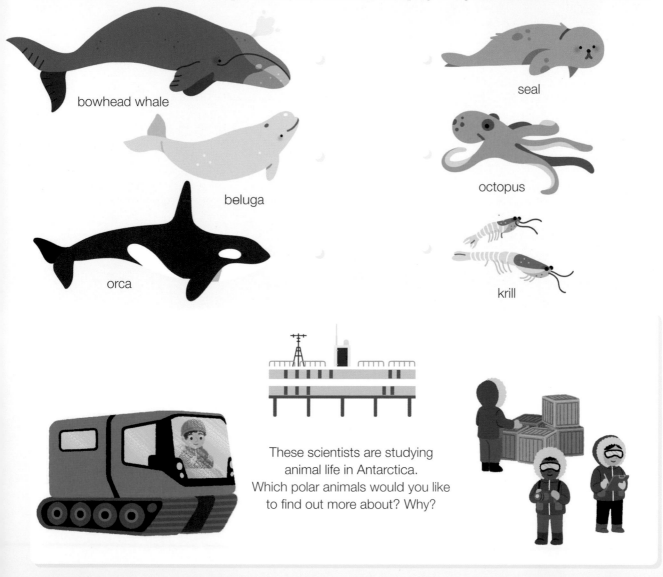

bowhead whale

seal

beluga

octopus

orca

krill

These scientists are studying animal life in Antarctica. Which polar animals would you like to find out more about? Why?

The Mountains
in the Winter

Up in the Himalayas

This mountain range in Asia includes the world's highest peaks. Many animals live in the Tibetan region.

golden eagle

Tibetan prayer flags

rocks

Chukar partridge: prefers to walk than to fly

high level ground

long horns

soft fur

male

female

Tibetan antelopes

carrying heavy loads

yaks

very thick hair

Himalayan vultures

Nomadic yak herders raise yaks for milk and meat.

feeding on dead animals

What
is a yeti

?

wild goat

easily climbing rocks to escape

snow leopards

snowy mountain meadow

living in large herds

kiang, or Tibetan wild ass

red panda: eats mostly bamboo

excellent climber

Have you seen a documentary or read about a creature called a yeti? Legend has it that this large, apelike being lives in the Himalayas.

While huge footprints have been seen, scientists think they were made by bears. Fossils of giant apes have been found too, but they died out 300,000 years ago.

As of now, no one knows if the yeti actually exists or is just an imaginary being, like the Loch Ness monster. What do you think?

Japanese Macaque

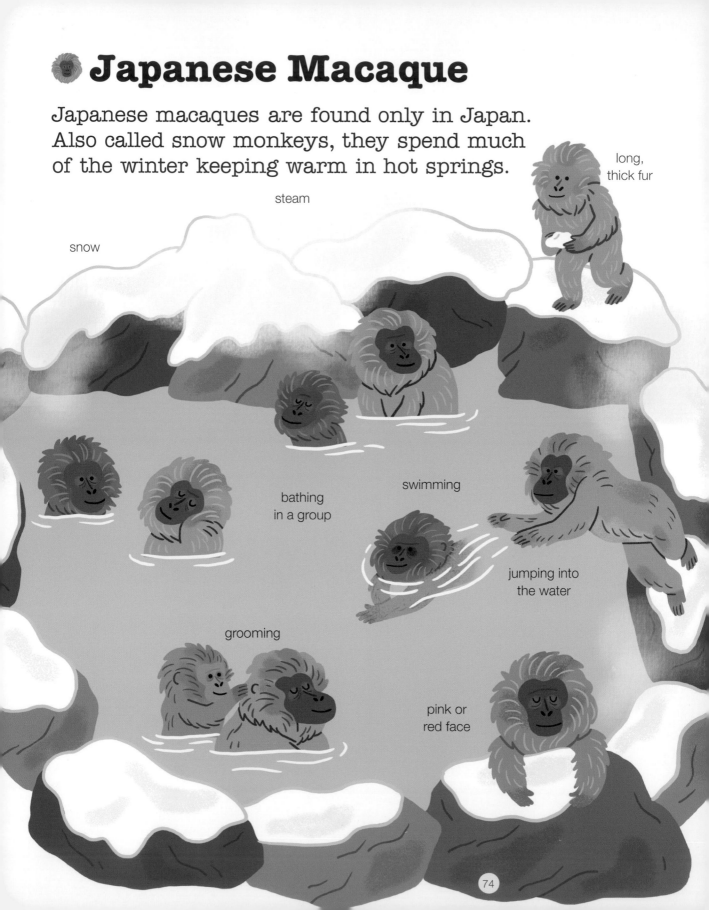

Japanese macaques are found only in Japan. Also called snow monkeys, they spend much of the winter keeping warm in hot springs.

long, thick fur

steam

snow

swimming

bathing in a group

jumping into the water

grooming

pink or red face

🐼 Giant Panda

Giant pandas, which are related to bears, are found mainly in the mountainous forests of central China.

Pandas are well-known for eating bamboo. It is their main source of food, and they spend more than half a day chewing on the shoots, stems, and leaves!

Their strong jaw muscles and large back teeth help them eat a lot of bamboo: up to 44 pounds (20 kilograms) a day.

On rare occasions, a giant panda may eat the remains of a small animal. And when they're not eating, they are sleeping!

claws

round ears

bamboo: stays green all winter

thick fur

expert climbers

munching on bamboo

sheltering from the wind and cold

🦙 In South America

On the plateaus of the Andes Mountains, the air is thinner and there is less oxygen. People and animals here are used to living at these high altitudes.

big eyes

feeding

guanacos

viscacha

coming down from snow-covered areas

Andean mountain cat

fine, soft fur

vicuñas

chinchillas

harvesting potatoes

having a dust bath

huge wings

Andean condor

llamas

thick, woolly coat

llama farmer

montero, a fringed hat

Quechua people

chullo, or woolly hat

weaving llama wool

poncho

sheep

In the mountains, it gets colder as you climb higher. The temperature falls about 5°F every 1,000 feet (or about 10°C every 1,000 meters).

Earth is heated by light from the Sun, and it is warmest at ground level. As hot air from the ground rises, it expands and cools.

However, the Sun's light is still strong up in the mountains. It's a good idea to protect your eyes and skin from ultraviolet, or UV, solar rays.

Fur and Feathers

In the winter, many animals that live in cold climates change their coats to keep warm or to camouflage against their snowy environment.

in summer

in winter

light coat

dark coat: easily absorbs heat

alpine chamois

grayish-brown coat

white coat for camouflage

mountain hare

brown and black spots on feathers

all-white feathers

ptarmigan

short coat

longer, thicker coat

red fox

in summer

sheep
farmer

shearing
sheep

freshly shorn
sheep

in winter

thick
wool fleece

taking sheep to graze

Why
do we shear sheep

?

Wool protects sheep from the cold. But it is always growing, and in the summer, the sheep get too warm.

This is the reason why sheep are sheared every spring. Shearing doesn't hurt them, and without their wool, the sheep are cleaner, healthier, and cooler.

Did you know that sheep's wool is so warm that it can even be used to insulate homes? What else do you think it can be used for?

Mountain Climbers **82**
Making Tracks **84**

 # Lynx

The lynx has long, soft fur to keep it warm in its cold and snowy habitat. Great eyesight and hearing also help this skilled hunter find prey.

The Alps

long tufts

forest

short, black-tipped tail

large paws that keep it from sinking into snow

can spot a mouse from far away

silently approaching a deer

climbs trees to escape from predators

🐭 Ermine

In the winter, ermine spend a lot of time in their burrows, coming out only when they need to look for food.

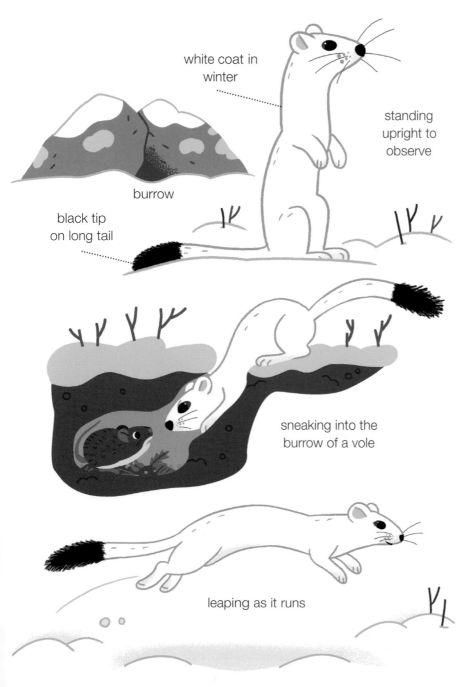

white coat in winter

standing upright to observe

burrow

black tip on long tail

sneaking into the burrow of a vole

leaping as it runs

In the summer, ermine have a brown-red coat. Gradually, as the seasons change and the weather gets colder, they turn all white... except the tips of their tails.

When an eagle spots an ermine and dives toward it, the little critter will wave its tail. The eagle will focus on the black tip of the tail and try to catch it.

The rest of the ermine is well-camouflaged against the snow. Its tail slips between the talons of the eagle as the ermine quickly scampers off.

⛰ Mountain Climbers

These mountain animals of the Alps in Europe are very agile. They can handle the rocky terrain.

alpine chamois

hook-shaped horns

The Alps

long hind legs

two-layer winter coat

sleeping in the snow

living in a herd

digging the ground for plants to eat

skier not bothering the animals

big horns

male

climbing a
steep slope

short horns

taking big
leaps

ibex

female

trying not to sink
in the snow

large,
curved horns

mouflons

In the winter, mouflons
move down the
mountain to look
for food.

How
do these
animals
climb

?

On the playground, you've
probably noticed that it isn't
easy to climb up equipment
while maintaining your balance.

The hooves of an alpine chamois
can grip the rocks well. Their
two toes spread apart or
squeeze together as they climb.

The ibex can jump more than
6 feet (1.8 meters) straight up
in the air. Also, their suction-
cup-like hooves have a firm hold
on the rocky cliffs.

Making Tracks

Who came this way? In the snow, animals leave traces of their movements. They may also mark their territories on purpose.

The Alps

black grouse droppings

ptarmigan feather

backcountry ski tracks

alpine chamois tracks

mountain hare fur

squirrel footprints

mountain hare footprints

Why

do wolves walk in single file ?

ptarmigan wing tracks

tracks of **wolves** walking one behind another

ermine tracks

ruffed grouse footprints

fox droppings

less snow because of climate change

Walking on soft, thick snow takes more effort than walking on hard, level ground. Animals use a lot more energy just to get around.

When they travel in single file, each wolf steps into the tracks of the wolf ahead of it. This makes walking less tiring.

Where have you walked in single file? Do you find it easier to move this way? Why or why not?

Fur and Feathers **78**
Hibernating and Overwintering **86**

Hibernating and Overwintering

In cold-climate regions, some animals spend their winters hibernating while others overwinter. It is their way of conserving energy when it is cold and when food is scarce.

hibernating

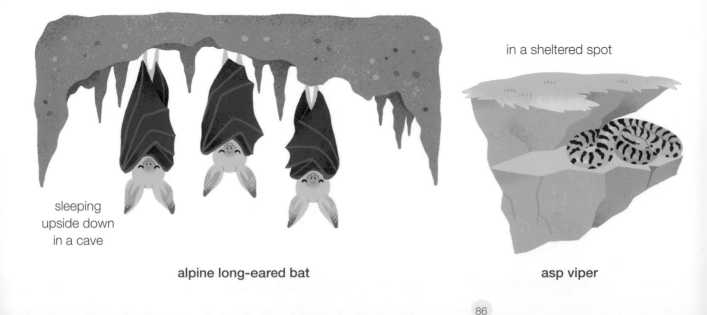

burrow

toilet

curled up on a bed of dry grass

marmots

sleeping upside down in a cave

alpine long-eared bat

in a sheltered spot

asp viper

overwintering

in the mud of a pond

common frog

in a group of thousands
between rocks

ladybugs

in a burrow

staying still
and going out
very little

black grouse

bottom of a lake

keeping still

arctic char

What
does it mean
to *hibernate*
and *overwinter*
?

When an animal, such as the marmot, hibernates, it sleeps deeply. Its body cools, and its heartbeat and breathing slow down.

Animals that overwinter, including the brown bear, reduce their activities and sleep lightly. They may venture out of their shelters for short periods.

However, the marmot does wake up several times during the winter, mostly to pee. They quickly return to hibernating.

Small Creatures **22**
Brown Bear **36**

⚠ Animals in Danger

Changes in climate affect plants and animals. The habitats of animals get smaller as plant life is lost, and they have to move in search of food and shelter.

thinner layer of snow

marmot: growing weaker and having fewer young

eagle: spotting its prey

mountain hare: keeping its white coat even when there's no snow

European hare: moving to the feeding ground of the mountain hare

Why
does climate change matter **?**

ptarmigan:
moving higher to
avoid the heat

melting
snow

forest
drying out

Animals that live in cold climates
will move to higher altitudes
to keep cool. There is less land
higher up, which means that the
animals' habitats are shrinking.

Animals that depend on plants
for food may not find the same
plants at higher altitudes. This
alters the diet of many animal
species, such as butterflies.

The balance of nature is
affected, and it is important to
ensure that plant and animal
species don't die out because of
something that is preventable.

SAVE THE
PLANET

Amur Tiger **42**
Polar Bear **52**

Let's Review!

The mountain hare and ptarmigan change color in the winter. What color will their fur and feathers be? What is the reason for this change?

What special features do each of these animals have to survive in their habitat?

In the winter, some animals hibernate or overwinter. Do you remember what the difference is between the two? Which of these animals are hibernating? Which ones are overwintering?

Who left these tracks? Match each set of footprints to the animal that made them.

What do your footprints look like?

Index

M

macaque 74
Magellanic penguin 61
maple 33
marine mammal 52, 54, 56–57
marmot 86, 87, 88
midge 58, 65
migration 40, 41
mink 35
monkey 74
montero 77
moose 24, 33, 38–39, 45
mouflon 83
mountain hare 78, 84, 88
mouse 80
musk ox 10, 18, 19, 25
muskrat 22

N

narwhal 50, 56, 57
nature reserve 43
nest 17, 22
North America 8, 10–11, 13, 53
northern goshawk 40
northern lights 25

O

oak 33
octopus 56, 62
oil rig 51
oil slick 51
omnivore 37
orca 57, 59, 63
overwintering 22–23, 37, 86–87
owl 11, 16, 17, 19, 25, 26, 45

P

pack ice 51, 53
paddle 39
penguin 55, 58, 60–61, 65, 67
phytoplankton 57
pika 22
pine 32, 33, 41,
pod 57
polar bear 50, 52–53, 66
polar lights 25
polar wolf 14–15
pollution 51, 59, 60
ptarmigan 78, 84–85, 89
puffin 55
pup 14, 67

Q

qiviut 19
Quechua people 76–77

R

rainbow 25
raven 17
razorbill 55
red crossbill 41, 44
red fox 21, 78
red panda 73
reindeer 12–13, 32, 44
research station 58, 59
right whale 26
rockhopper penguin 61
ruffed grouse 16, 18, 85

S

sable 33, 35
salmon 11, 36
Sámi people 13
scientist 58, 59
seabird 27, 55, 57
seal 11, 52, 53, 57, 59, 62–63, 64, 67
seasonal coat change 78–79
shearing 79
sheep 77, 79
shellfish 54
shrimp 61, 62
Siberia 9
Siberian grouse 40
Siberian jay 41
Siberian lynx 32, 45
Siberian musk deer 32, 45
Siberian nuthatch 41
Siberian weasel 35
silver birch 10, 33
skua 55, 59
sled dog 10
snow goose 17
snow leopard 73
snowmobile 11, 32
snow monkey 74
snowpack 10
snowy owl 11, 16, 17, 19, 25, 26
South America 8, 76–77
spruce 33
squid 59, 62
squirrel 23, 84
Steller sea lion 50
swarm 57

T

taiga 9, 32, 36
taiga flycatcher 41
talon 16–17
tamarack 33
tern 27, 51, 59
Tibet, China 72, 73
Tibetan antelope 72
Tibetan prayer flag 72
Tibetan wild ass 73
tiger 32, 37, 42–43, 44
tracks 84–85
trapper 33
tundra 8, 11, 16–17
tusk 54, 57

V

vibrissae 54, 62
vicuña 76
viscacha 76
vole 81
vulture 72

W

walrus 51, 54, 66
weasel 33, 34, 35
Weddell seal 59, 62–63, 67
whale 26, 50, 56, 57, 66
white wolf 14–15
wild boar 42
wild goat 73
wolf 10, 13, 14–15, 17, 19, 25, 26, 85
wolverine 33, 34, 44
woodcutter 33
wool 77, 79

Y

yak 72
Yakut people 32
yeti 73

DO YOU KNOW?™ series

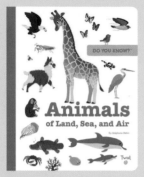

978-2-40803-356-9

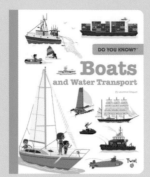

978-2-40804-255-4

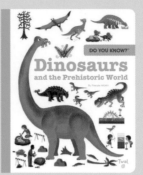

978-2-40802-467-3

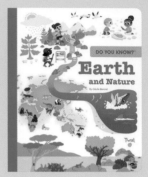

978-2-40803-357-6

978-2-40803-753-6

978-2-40804-253-0

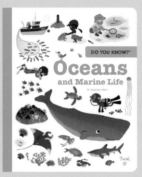

978-2-40802-466-6

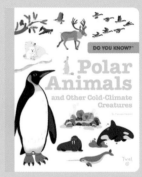

978-2-40804-620-0

978-2-40802-916-6

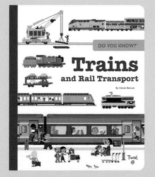

978-2-40803-755-0

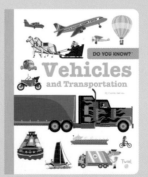

978-2-40802-915-9